GEARED FOR GROWTH BIBLE STUDIES

MESSENGER OF LOVE

A STUDY IN MALACHI

BIBLE STUDIES TO IMPACT THE LIVES OF ORDINARY PEOPLE

Christian Focus Publications

The Word Worldwide

Written by Marie Dinnen

For details of our titles visit us on our website
www.christianfocus.com

ISBN 1-85792-885-7

Copyright © WEC International

Published in 2003 by
Christian Focus Publications, Geanies House,
Fearn, Ross-shire, IV20 ITW, Scotland
and
WEC International, Bulstrode, Oxford Road,
Gerrards Cross, Bucks, SL9 8SZ

Cover design by Alister MacInnes

Printed and bound by J W Arrowsmith, Bristol

CONTENTS

QUESTIONS AND NOTES

ANSWER GUIDE

PREFACE

GEARED FOR GROWTH

**'Where there's LIFE there's GROWTH:
Where there's GROWTH there's LIFE.'**

WHY GROW a study group?

Because as we study the Bible and share together we can

- learn to combat loneliness, depression, staleness, frustration, and other problems
- get to understand and love each other
- become responsive to the Holy Spirit's dealing and obedient to God's Word

and that's GROWTH.

How do you GROW a study group?

- Just start by asking a friend to join you and then aim at expanding your group.
- Study the set portions daily (they are brief and easy: no catches).
- Meet once a week to discuss what you find.
- Befriend others, both Christians and non Christians, and work away together

see how it GROWS!

WHEN you GROW ...

This will happen at school, at home, at work, at play, in your youth group, your student fellowship, women's meetings, mid-week meetings, churches and communities,

you'll be REACHING THROUGH TEACHING

INTRODUCTORY STUDY

1. Suppose you are talking to a friend who recently has had to cope with heartbreak and trouble. By way of comfort, you say: 'Even though things have been hard, remember, God loves you.'

But your friend says, 'You must be joking! How can you say God loves me when all this has happened? The way I look at it, if God loved me at all, He would have stepped in and prevented me having it so rough.'

How would you reply?

2. You are speaking to your teenage son about the fact that he only goes to church with you because it is expected of him, and once the service is over, he lives the rest of the week as he pleases. You say, 'You know, son, that's really giving God the cold shoulder. It's showing you don't care about Him.' Son says, 'Well, I like that! You say I don't care about God. How come? You should talk to some of my mates, they think I'm terribly religious because I go to church. Honestly, though, if I do that much, haven't I done my bit?'

How would you answer?

3. Anna is a deserted wife who is living with another man. She comes to your Bible Study group and is learning what it means to be a Christian. She has lots of problems, and you encourage her to pray about them and ask God's help. One day she comes to you, exasperated, and says: 'It doesn't work! I've pleaded with God, I've even been in tears as I prayed. I've done everything you said ... and God hasn't heard my prayers. Why doesn't He answer?'

What would you say?

4. In a discussion about world events, the question arises: 'When there is so much corruption around, even in the leaders of nations – where does God fit into the picture? How is it that these men can get away with it? Is God not a God of justice?'

What would your comment be?

5. After hearing a tape by a noted speaker, a friend returns it to you, saying: 'Thanks very much, I enjoyed it. Of course all this "forgiveness" bit doesn't apply to me. Being a Christian, I live a good life and love my neighbour and even put my £5 regularly in the plate each Sunday! And I didn't quite get the bit about

cheating God of what is rightfully His. What did that mean?' What would you say to your friend?

6. Someone is explaining to you what he believes. He says: 'In our day and generation, we have come to realise that a lot of myth has been mixed with the actual history written in the Bible. For example, the miracles of Christ can now be readily and scientifically explained, and such ideas as the virgin birth and the bodily resurrection of Jesus are quite obviously just exaggerations of the original story.' 'But,' you protest, 'these are pretty strong accusations to make against Christ Jesus.' To which he replies: 'Now, wait a minute! Don't get me wrong. I'm not saying anything against Jesus Himself. He was a great man, and His teachings are among the finest in the world. It's just the Bible that is – well – a bit out of date, and there are things in it that today's intellectuals cannot accept.'
How would you continue?

God tells us in His Word that we should be ready at all times to answer anyone who asks about our faith. God is counting on every Christian to be His messenger to the people round about, and we can often share our faith quietly and confidently in everyday situations.
Four hundred years before the birth of Christ, God sent His messenger, Malachi, to challenge the people of his day. The name 'Malachi' simply means 'messenger.'
Compare the following references with the situations you have been discussing, and perhaps you will be surprised at how little human nature has changed over the years!

Situation	I.	Malachi	1:2
	2		1:6-8
	3.		2:13-14
	4.		2:17
	5.		3:7-10
	6.		3:13

The people in Malachi's day were disobeying God, and yet were oblivious of the seriousness of their sin. During these studies, ask the Lord to give you opportunities to share your faith with the people you meet, those who don't realize how far away from God they are.
Find out what God wants for the people who live in your street, who go to your college, who work in your office or shop, or whose lives touch yours in any way – by reading Malachi 3:16-18.

STUDY 1

GOD'S LOVE REPUDIATED

QUESTIONS

DAY 1 *Malachi 1:1-6.*
a) What does the name Malachi mean?
b) Whose word was he to give?
c) To whom was the message given?

DAY 2 *Malachi 1:2.*
a) What did God say to show His people He cared for them?
b) What question would have grieved the heart of God?
c) What was the Lord's answer?

DAY 3 *Malachi 1:2-3; Genesis 32:24-30; Hebrews 11:20.*
a) Do you think that God was unfair in loving Jacob? Why?
b) Why was God unable to bless Esau in the same way?

DAY 4 *Malachi 1:3-4; Genesis 25:31-34; Deuteronomy 21:17.*
a) What happens to those who reject God's gift of salvation today?
b) What do you think the 'birthright' in Genesis means?

DAY 5 *Malachi 1:3-4.*
a) What became of Esau's inheritance?
b) Read Ezekiel 35:1-9. Why did Esau's descendants, the Edomites, also suffer?

DAY 6 *Malachi 1:4-5.*
a) Do you think God was unjust towards the Edomites?
b) God has set His love on you. How does that make you feel? (Acts 13:48; Eph. 1:4-6)

DAY 7 *Malachi 1:5-6.*
a) How was God's love demonstrated to the Israelites?
b) Do we blame God when the way is difficult?
c) Has God promised that things will always be easy for His people (2 Tim. 3:10-13)?

Share some of the ways in which these verses have been true for you.

NOTES

In this first section of Malachi we see God's love questioned and repudiated.

Malachi was chosen by God for a very difficult task. He had to plead with God's people to return and truly worship Him, so that God could bless them as He had promised.

Their response showed how out of touch with God and His law they really were: 'How have YOU loved us?' they said. Satan delights in trying to blind the eyes of God's children. It is only as we walk in love and responsive obedience that we are capable of 'counting our blessings' and seeing God's loving hand in our lives. How surely and certainly the Spirit of God reveals God and His love to the responsive heart. The hymn writer puts it:

> Loved with everlasting love,
> Led by grace that love to know,
> Spirit breathing from above,
> Thou has taught me it is so,
> Oh this full and perfect peace!
> Oh this transport all Divine!
> In a love that cannot cease,
> I am His and He is mine.

God's love is clearly seen by those who obey Him. Look up Jeremiah 31:3 and Deuteronomy 7:7-8.

God could not bless Esau because he rejected the gift God had given him. In the same way God could not bless Israel because they spurned His love.

Edom said, 'We will rebuild the ruins,' i.e. 'We'll go it alone. See if we don't make a success of it without You.' Isn't this the picture of a heart at variance with the Almighty? Do you ever find yourself doing your own thing your own way because you are really at variance with what God wants you to do?

God's reply to Edom's defiance was: 'You may build. But it will all be brought to nothing.'

How much we need to learn to walk in obedience to the will of God. He loves us. Even if we cannot see where the circumstances of life are leading us, let us 'trust and obey' Him. When He plans our ways and works out the problems, He always does so with our good and His blessing in view.

The Living Bible, in Romans 8:28 says, 'And we know that all that happens to us is working out for our good if we love God and are fitting into HIS PLANS.'

STUDY 2
SECOND-RATE SERVICE

QUESTIONS

DAY 1 *Malachi 1:6-7.*
a) Whom should a servant and a son, respect?
b) How did the priests despise God's name?

DAY 2 *Malachi 1:7-8; Hosea 4:9; Acts 5:1-5.*
a) Who was to blame for these blemished sacrifices? Why?
b) In what ways today can people bring unworthy offerings?

DAY 3 *Malachi 1:7-8.*
a) How can we despise God's table (1 Cor. 11:27-29)?
b) Why was their offering unacceptable to God?
c) Do you think a Governor would be honoured if offered a battered old gift?

DAY 4 *Malachi 1:9.*
a) What does God consider important when we give to Him (2 Cor. 8:12)?
b) What kind of people should we be looking for to pray with us and for us (Acts 9:10-18; 12:12-16)?
c) When we cry to God for forgiveness, does He hear and forgive (Acts 16:30-34; 1 John 1:9)?

DAY 5 *Malachi 1:10-11.*
a) Why did God have no pleasure in the Israelites' offerings?
b) What kind of service does God ask of us (Rom. 12:1; 1 Pet. 5:2; Judg. 5:2-9)?

DAY 6 *Malachi 1:11; Revelation 5:8-9.*
a) Where will God's people ultimately be gathered from?
b) What does incense symbolise for us?
c) In whose name should prayer be made (John 14:13-14)?

DAY 7 *Malachi 1:11.*
a) Do we honour the name of Jesus by confessing Him before others? (See Rom. 20:9; 14:11; Phil. 2:11.)
b) Have you set aside time to pray daily?
c) Can you share any answers to prayer you have had?

NOTES

God made it perfectly clear to Israel as to the standards His holiness required. He had stipulated three things:

Offerings made to God must be 'without defect' (Exod. 12:5; Lev. 1:3; Deut. 17:1 and many other references).
Priests who served in the temple must be 'holy' (Lev. 21:6).
People who represent the Church of God must be 'holy and without blemish' (Lev. 11:44, 45; Eph. 5:27).

In type, the offering foreshadowed the Lamb of God who would be offered for the sin of the world (1 Pet. 1:19). The priest typified our Great High Priest, Jesus Himself, who ever lives to make intercession for us (Heb. 2:17; 7:25). The people (Israel) were stumbled because they saw corruption amongst the priests, but priests and people alike were guilty before God in the offering of less than perfect sacrifices.

We should stop and consider what our service and offerings are like. Do we offer Him freely all that we have and are, or do we give Him the 'leftovers' of our time, possessions, ourselves, etc.?

The Israelites were impatient. They could see no sign of God's promised Messiah. So they took matters into their own hands. They started to live for themselves instead of God. Do we grow weary of waiting for God's answers? Are we consistent and persistent in prayer? Do we ask others to pray with us when we begin to doubt or waver? How long did someone pray for you before you found salvation in Christ?

The hymn writer gives us good advice:

'Take time to be holy, speak oft with thy Lord,
Abide in Him always, and feed on His Word.
Make friends of God's children,
Help those who are weak,
Forgetting in nothing, His blessing to seek.'

And don't forget, prayer and praise go together (Phil. 4:6). When we cultivate the habit of taking everything to God in prayer, when we keep busy counting our blessings and praising the One who blesses, we won't have time to give way to doubt, despair or impatience. And the evil one won't find a loophole to get in with discouragement.

STUDY 3
THE WORKER AND HIS MESSAGE

QUESTIONS

DAY 1 *Malachi 1:12-13; Exodus 20:7.*
a) How is God's name profaned and what are the consequences? (See also Ezek. 36:23; Deut. 5:11.)
b) What made the priests weary of their service?
c) What are some of the things that discourage you in your Christian life?

DAY 2 *Malachi 1:14; Numbers 30:1-2; Ecclesiastes 5:4-5.*
a) How important is it to keep a vow you made to God?
b) Was the offering of a blemished sacrifice in keeping with the vow made?
c) How widely is God's name to be feared?

DAY 3 *Malachi 2:1-2; I Timothy 3:1-7.*
a) What should be the aim of all who serve God?
b) Read Romans 6:16-18. Whom do we serve?
c) Why will ministers and Christian workers be severely judged (I Pet. 4:17)?

DAY 4 *Malachi 2:3 (read in several versions).*
a) Who besides the priests suffered punishment?
b) What was the punishment (Gen. 4:16. See also Ps. 51:11)?
c) Who can remain in God's presence (Ps. 140:13; Exod. 33:14-17)?

DAY 5 *Malachi 2:4-7.*
a) To whom did God give His commandments?
b) Should we expect our ministers and Christian teachers to teach us God's Word?
c) What do you think Jesus meant when He told Peter to 'Feed my lambs' and 'Feed my sheep' (John 21:15-17)?

QUESTIONS (contd.)

DAY 6 *Malachi 2:5-6 (read in several versions).*
a) What was the priests' message to be?
b) Does it matter if what we say and how we live don't match up? Read Paul's desire in I Corinthians 9:24-27 and make it yours.

DAY 7 *Malachi 2:7-9.*
a) Why does God's judgement fall first on his own people (I Pet. 1:15-16; 4:17)?
b) Discuss what can turn people away from God today.
c) Read Matthew 28:18-20. What do these verses say about our duty as Christians?

NOTES

The Christian worker and his message are both important to God. He takes great pains and gives detailed instruction to prepare His children to live and work for Him.

Moses was 40 years in the desert in preparation for the time when God would use him to lead the Israelites out of Egypt.

Paul spent three years in seclusion with God before he launched out into his God-given service (Gal. 1:17-18).

The priests were trained from generation to generation in their holy duties. When they started to accept and offer blemished animals in sacrifice, they did so in the full knowledge that they were contravening God's laws.

This is a challenge to us not to offer anything less than our best in gifts and service to Him. Read I Peter 4:17 again. No wonder the priests were tired of their job. Have you not experienced the weariness of trying to do something you are half-hearted about? What a difference when we get into a job we are enthusiastic about. It is done in no time. This is the glad, joyful, obedient service that God wants of us. This kind of service brings not only eternal reward and life for others, but deeper joy to the one who serves.

Note, too, that just as the people were affected by the priests' sinfulness, so sin in our lives can affect others. In Acts 5:1-10 we see that God not only had to deal drastically with Ananias and Sapphira because of their deceit, but also that 'Great fear seized the whole church'.

Speaking to the nation of Israel, God said, 'The heathen shall believe when I am sanctified in you before their eyes' (Ezek. 36:23).

Paul earnestly prayed that his life would measure up to what he taught. His objective for his converts is embodied in I Peter 3:2-4, namely, that their lives would show forth Christ. Is this how you live, how you want to live, that others might believe?

STUDY 4
FAITHLESSNESS TO GOD AND MAN

QUESTIONS

DAY 1 *Malachi 2:10-11; 2 Corinthians 6:14-17.*
a) What do you learn from these two references about Christian marriage?
b) Discuss some of the complications which arise when a Christian marries a non-Christian.

DAY 2 *Malachi 2:11-12; 1 Kings 11:1-2.*
a) If one partner in marriage is converted after marriage, should he/she leave the unconverted partner (1 Cor. 7:12-15)?
b) Why did God command that His children were not to marry unbelievers?

DAY 3 *Malachi 2:13-15.*
a) Why did God not accept the offerings the people brought?
b) Why did God oppose divorce (Gen. 2:24; Matt. 5:32)?

DAY 4 *Malachi 2:15-17; Genesis 2:24; Matthew 19:4-6.*
a) What have you discovered about God's view of divorce?
b) Do Psalm 127:3 and Proverbs 22:6 give any directive about the children of an insecure marriage?

DAY 5 *Malachi 2:17; Isaiah 5:20.*
a) What 'wearied' God?
b) What attitudes and behaviour might cause us to 'weary' God?

DAY 6 *Malachi 2:17; 1 John 1:5-9; John 3:16.*
a) Will God really punish those who do evil (Rev. 21:7-8)?
b) What provision has God made for us when we sin?

DAY 7 *Malachi 2:10-17.*
a) Have you had new insights into God's Word in this week's study?
b) What practical things have you learned?

NOTES

Background reading to this chapter tells us that immorality abounded amongst all classes in Israel at this time. Adultery, perjury, fraud and oppression of the poor was rife. God, however, speaks through Malachi mainly against the mixed marriages, unfaithfulness and divorce at this juncture.

The Word of God leaves us in no doubt that mixed marriages are against the law of God. Here, the issue is not one of difference of colour, but of faith. 'Do not be mismated with unbelievers' is the Word of God to Christians (2 Cor. 6:14). As Jews, the Israelites were to marry Jews. Why? Because marriage with a non-believer would lead to weakening of faith, and God's people would be led into compromise and eventually idolatry.

God had covenanted to be the God of Israel. Israel's response was that they would be His people. To maintain this relationship they had to marry within the nation. Those who deliberately broke this covenant were really despising God Himself.

God wanted Jewish men with Jewish wives so that their children might be reared in faithfulness and obedience to God. Through the Jewish line the Messiah Himself would one day come.

The issue of divorce was also against the law of God. His Word makes it abundantly clear that Christians are to marry Christians. In an 'unsaved' marriage should one become a Christian, God decrees that the Christian partner should remain true to the marriage vows, and so live Christ in the home that the unbelieving partner will be won.

The secure Christian marriage provides the right climate in which children can be reared to love, trust and obey God.

There is much for us to learn from the issues discussed this week. Look over some of the references again and be sure your marriage is built on God's pattern. In these days when many look so lightly on their marriage vows, be sure of what you believe, and be able to use the Word of God with others who are finding problems on this level.

STUDY 5

CONFRONTATION

QUESTIONS

DAY 1 *Malachi 3:1; Matthew 11:10; 1 Corinthians 6:19.*
a) Who was God's messenger and what was his ministry?
b) What would the Lord do at His coming (Hag. 2:7)?
c) Has this any meaning for us today?

DAY 2 *Malachi 3:2-3; 1 John 2:28; John 5:28-29.*
a) Discuss the importance of being ready, and the folly of not being ready, for Christ's return.
b) The silversmith uses fire to purify silver. How does God test His children?

DAY 3 *Malachi 3:2-3; Deuteronomy 18:5-7; 1 Peter 2:9-10.*
a) What was the task assigned to the tribe of Levi?
b) How are we involved as priests of God (Heb. 13:15-16; Phil. 4:18; Ps. 27:6; 51:17)?

DAY 4 *Malachi 3:3-4; Romans 12:1.*
a) Why did the priests need cleansing?
b) What does God want from us once we are His?

DAY 5 *Malachi 3:4-5; John 4:20-23; Revelation 21:8; 22:15.*
a) Why is Jerusalem so important to the Jews?
b) Read Deuteronomy 18:9-12. Why did God warn the Jews against sorcerers, etc.?
c) What happens to those who knowingly disobey God?

DAY 6 *Malachi 3:5; Psalm 82:1-4; 89:7.*
a) What does God say He will do when one person defrauds another?
b) Discuss what it means to 'fear' God.

DAY 7 *Malachi 3:6-7; Hebrews 13:8; James 1:17.*
a) What has Malachi 3:6 in common with the other references?
b) Does God change His standards to suit the current mood of the world (Num. 23:19; Titus 1:2-3)?
c) How would you answer someone who said, 'If God is all-loving, how can He cast anyone out from His presence (2 Pet. 3:9; Hos. 14:1-2)?'

NOTES

'Confrontation' is a word much used today in a political sense. Here in Malachi we find it used on a spiritual level. God is facing His people up and pointing out where they fall far short of His glory. While 'the temple' in this portion is taken to mean the actual building in Jerusalem, Paul uses it in the sense that our bodies are the temple of the living God and we need to yield to His cleansing and control. The implication, however, is to the Lord's second coming and the warning rings loud and clear that we are to be ready now, because we don't know just when Christ will come again.

The illustration of the local silversmith is graphically used to apply a spiritual principle. The silversmith places raw silver rock into his large metal cauldron and lights a fire underneath. The metal, useless in its raw state, is exposed to intense heat day and night, and under the heat the rock breaks up and is finally reduced to a molten liquid. This is brought to the boil so that the impurities are brought to the surface and are skimmed off by the silversmith. This process of intense heat and skimming off is repeated until no impurities remain and the silversmith can see himself reflected in the liquid silver.

Malachi's message would be clearly understood by all those familiar with the work of the silversmith. The Messiah sits today as a refiner of His people. He applies the heat and pressure of the problems and trials of life to His children. This forces the hidden impurities of our characters and behaviour up to the conscious level, where God deals with them (as we confess our need) until at last He can see a perfect reflection of Himself in His children.

Although this section deals only with the purifying of the 'sons of Levi', i.e., the priesthood, yet because everyone who comes to faith in Christ is made a priest of God, this whole message applies most definitely to each of us today.

The verses on judgement are very solemn ones. Yet God abundantly provided for us that we might be cleansed and keep on walking as cleansed people, a people in whom He can delight. Stephen said to the Jews, 'You stiff-necked and uncircumcised in heart and ears, ye do always resist the Spirit: as your fathers did, so do you' (Acts 7:51). This was certainly true of Israel in Malachi's day, and is startlingly true of our present day.

But God in His longsuffering ever yearns over His backslidden children and continually pleads with them to return. Remember how He said through Paul in Galatians 4:19, 'Oh my children, how you are hurting me! I am once again suffering for you the pains of a mother in childbirth – longing for the time when you will be finally filled with Christ.'

Let us make sure that we receive His grace which delivers us from judgement, and that in no way are we kicking against God's purifying work in our lives, thus causing Him to suffer afresh.

A recent song writer puts it this way, referring to the work of God's Spirit in our lives:

> Purify my heart,
> Let me be as gold and precious silver.
> Purify my heart,
> Let me be as gold, pure gold.
> Refiner's fire, my heart's one desire,
> Is to be holy,
> Set aside for you Lord.
> I choose to be holy,
> Set aside for you my Master,
> Ready to do your will.

STUDY 6
ROBBING GOD

QUESTIONS

DAY 1 *Malachi 3:8; Leviticus 27:30-32; Deuteronomy 12:6.*
    a) What is meant by 'robbing' God (Acts 2:44-45; Eph. 4:28)?
    b) Do you know the difference between tithes and offerings?

DAY 2 *Malachi 3:9; Deuteronomy 23:5; Isaiah 1:19-20.*
    a) What happens to those who rob God?
    b) What happens to those who are obedient to Him?

DAY 3 *Malachi 3:10; Nehemiah 13:5; Hosea 6:3.*
    a) Where and for what reason were the people to give?
    b) What happens to those who put God to the test (i.e., are obedient in giving)?

DAY 4 *Malachi 3:10-11; Philippians 4:19.*
    a) What do these verses say about the generosity of God?
    b) Share with your group ways in which God has blessed you.

DAY 5 *Malachi 3:11; Joel 2:23-26; John 15:8,16.*
    a) What will God do for those who live in obedience to Him?
    b) What does this mean for the Christian?

DAY 6 *Malachi 3:11-12; Joel 2:2-3; Isaiah 35:1-2.*
    a) What do the locusts do to the crops and what does God do about it?
    b) Who is the 'LORD Almighty' (Ps. 46:10-11; Luke 2:13 in RSV)?

DAY 7 *Malachi 3:12-13; Matthew 12:36; Jude 14-16. Read these references in several versions.*
    a) How did the people show they had lost touch with God?
    b) Why are the words we speak so important?

NOTES

Malachi in these verses deals with the failure of the Israelites in giving to God as He had instructed them. Not only now, but through the generations, there had been a withholding of the 'tithes'. God had ordained that those who earned an income (i.e., produced crops and herds) would give in such a way that the priests (who were too busy doing God's work in the temple) would be provided for. Repentance and amendment of their ways would bring God's abundant blessing. In verse 6 Malachi terms the Israelites 'sons of Jacob'. In the same way as Jacob had deceived his father and cheated his brother, so were they robbing God. Times had been hard and the Israelites had been through periods of famine, but God declared that if they would just continue in obedience, giving as He had commanded, He would give back in abundance to them.

This is a spiritual principle. Read Luke 6:38, 'Give and it shall be given unto you.' The widow and her son gave what little they could spare in time of famine. Read what happened to them in I Kings 17:13-16.

The barrenness of famine made living hard for the Israelites. But God was trying to convince them of their spiritual barrenness brought about by disobedience. If they started to set their spiritual lives in order and to walk as God wanted them to in dependence upon Him, He would rectify things. The picture of the outpouring of abundant water and production of an abundant harvest shows us that God's plan is to shower spiritual provision on His children so that their lives will be productive and fruitful for Him.

Make the following verse of a well known hymn your prayer today.

> Were the whole realm of nature mine
> That were an offering far too small.
> Love so amazing, so divine,
> Shall have my soul, my life, my all.'

STUDY 7
CONTRASTS

QUESTIONS

DAY 1 *Malachi 3:13-16; Psalm 1.*
    a) Discuss the two different heart attitudes shown in Malachi 3 vv. 13, 16.
    b) Why did the Israelites say it was vain or futile to serve God?
    c) What is God's promise to those who do live for Him?

DAY 2 *Malachi 3:15; Psalm 31:23; 37:7-13.*
    a) Do you think the arrogant and proud are really happy?
    b) Do the wicked really prosper?

DAY 3 *Malachi 3:16.*
    a) What were these people talking about?
    b) Can we be like these people?
    c) Is Psalm 141:3 your prayer?

DAY 4 *Malachi 3:16; Revelation 20:12,15.*
    a) How can you be sure that your name is written in God's book of life?
    b) Can you rewrite this phrase, 'for them that feared the Lord and honoured His name' in your own words?

DAY 5 *Malachi 3:17; 1 Corinthians 6:19-20; 1 Thessalonians 4:16-17.*
    a) Who owns you?
    b) When will the Lord make up His 'treasured possession'?

DAY 6 *Malachi 3:17-18; Psalm 103:13.*
    a) Who will God 'spare', that is, be merciful to?
    b) There are two kinds of people spoken of here. Who are they?

DAY 7 *Malachi 4:1; 2 Thessalonians 1:7-8; Revelation 21:8.*
    a) What is 'the day' spoken of here?
    b) What will happen to those who have not trusted Christ?

NOTES

In this portion of Malachi we can almost visualise the Israelites in little huddles, moaning and complaining to each other that it is useless to serve God. Why, the heathen nations round about seem to be well off and enjoying themselves and they don't bother with Jehovah!

However, Malachi has something very clear and definite to say about this state of affairs. He does not think purely of the physical and material comforts of life. He looks beyond to a day of reckoning when Christ will return to judge the world. He contrasts the state of those who really love and serve God with that of those who have rejected Him.

Look up Revelation 7:12-17.

Those who have received Christ and lived for Him on earth – those whose names are in the Book of Life:

1. Will serve God day and night in His temple.
2. Will never hunger or thirst again.
3. Will be protected by their Shepherd, the Lamb of God.
4. Will be led by the Lamb of God to springs of living waters.
5. Will have all tears wiped away by God.
6. Will be with the Lord forever.

The wicked who refused to accept God's way of salvation, whose names are not written in the Lamb's book of life, will be thrown into the lake of fire. Look up Revelation 20:10-15; 21:8. This is spoken of as suffering the 'second death'. Matthew 10:28 indicates that the death of our physical body is one thing, but the destruction of the soul is another. For the Christian, physical death is the doorway into God's eternal presence. He will never experience spiritual death. But for the unbeliever there is no hope once Christ comes. He will be cut off eternally from the presence of God. We can scarcely imagine what it will mean to be cut off from all influences for good, happiness, joy and beauty, and to be cast out into darkness where there is no God, and no hope.

This chapter sounds a fearful warning note for us to surrender to Christ now and be His for time and all eternity.

STUDY 8
MESSIAH'S SECOND COMING

QUESTIONS

DAY 1 a) Share with your group something that has impressed you in the studies so far.
b) Read Malachi 4:1; 2 Thessalonians 1:5-10. How do you feel about these verses?

DAY 2 *Malachi 4:2.*
a) To whom will the Son of Righteousness come?
b) What does this verse say He will be like?
c) When He returns, what will we be like (1 John 3:2)?

DAY 3 *Malachi 4:2-3.*
a) Who will tread the wicked underfoot?
b) Will the wicked not always flourish (Ps. 92:6-7)?

DAY 4 *Malachi 4:3-4.*
a) Are the laws, given by God to Moses, still binding on Christians today (Matt. 15:3-6; Mark 10:19-21)?
b) Why is this so?

DAY 5 *Malachi 4:5; Matthew 17:10-13; Luke 1:13,17.*
a) Who was the 'Elijah' of the New Testament (1 Kings 18:21, 39; Matt. 3:1-3)?
b) What was the message of these two men?

DAY 6 *Malachi 4:5-6; Luke 1:17.*
a) Who were to be reconciled to each other through the preaching of the messenger?
b) What was Jesus' comment on John the Baptist (Matt. 11:10-11)?

DAY 7 *Read Malachi 4:6 in several versions.*
a) When did God first curse the earth (Gen. 3:17-18)?
b) What was the result?
c) When will this curse be removed (Rev. 21:1-4)?

NOTES

The unbeliever, if he thinks about it at all, sees the Christian as a gullible fool waiting for God who is not really there, and who will never come to rescue His feeble followers.

But this is not what the Bible tells us of the Almighty God, the Creator who is the source of all power and wisdom and riches and strength and honour and glory and blessing.

It is an exciting experience to know God as Saviour and to be living each day in the thrilling expectation that He will return at any time. And that moment will surely come when our Lord Jesus will fulfil the promise 'I will come again'. That coming will be the climax and culmination of His redemptive work and the Lord will usher in that Kingdom where God is all in all. Read I Corinthians 15:23-28 in the Living Bible.

There are two things we must be very earnest about till that day.

The first is to be very sure we know Christ as our Saviour and Lord, and that we are growing day by day as we put into practice the things His Word tells us to do.

The second is to be concerned for others who are blind to their need of Christ, and diligently work and pray to extend Christ's Kingdom while there is yet time.

Remember there will be no second chance when Christ comes again. We must be prepared and ready NOW.

Read some of the verses that tell of Christ's coming: Acts 1:11; I Thessalonians 4:16; James 5:8; 2 Peter 3:12.

Don't you get excited and eager when you read verses like Matthew 24:30? 'They will see the Son of Man coming in the clouds of heaven with power and great glory.'

Can you say from a heart at peace with God, 'Even so, come, Lord Jesus' (Rev. 22:20)?

STUDY 9
GOD'S VIEW OF MARRIAGE AND DIVORCE

QUESTIONS

DAY 1 *Malachi 2:11; Ephesians 5:31-32; Revelation 19:7.*
a) Is Malachi 2:11 significant for us today?
b) To what is our relationship with Christ likened?

DAY 2 *Malachi 2:11; Ezra 9:12.*
a) To whom was Judah joined?
b) Discuss how Christians can get involved in wrong relationships.

DAY 3 *Malachi 2:11-13; I Samuel 15:22-24.*
a) Why were these offerings unacceptable to God?
b) Why didn't the Lord acknowledge their tears and bless them?

DAY 4 *Malachi 2:14-16; Matthew 19:1-12 (in several versions).*
a) What were these Jewish people doing?
b) Discuss what the Bible says about marriage and divorce. (See Gen. 2:24; I Cor. 7:2, 10-13, etc.)

DAY 5 *Luke 3:19-20; Leviticus 20:10.*
a) Why did John the Baptist condemn Herod?
b) Why shouldn't he have married Herodias?
c) How seriously does God look upon adultery?

DAY 6 *I John 1:7-9.*
a) Does God classify sin, i.e., is one sin worse than another?
b) On what grounds does God forgive any sin?

DAY 7 *John 8:3-11; Matthew 5:28-29.*
a) How did Jesus react to the men who accused this woman?
b) What made them leave without pressing their charges?

Commitment to marriage is generally very low these days. Broken homes are on the increase and there is a strong plea for directive regarding children of broken marriages.

Marriage, however, is a God-ordained sacrament. When people recognise this and give heed to what God says in His Word about the duties of marriage partners to each other, and when they follow the guidelines for rearing children in the 'nurture and admonition' ('training and instruction' NIV) of the Lord, then only blessing can result.

This week we have looked at the last few verses of Malachi chapter 2 and some related references, and sought to get an overview on marriage and divorce from the Bible.

The men of Israel who put away their own wives and sought partnerships with heathen women, were certainly breaking God's law. Their tears, far from being tears of repentance, were the expression of their obstinacy and self-centredness. Like spoilt children, they were crying for what they couldn't get without the corrective spanking they needed.

Psalm 34:18 is the remedy for their problem. God wanted to bless them. But He couldn't until He saw genuine repentance and brokenness on their part.

They had looked lightly on their marriage vows and failed to follow God's directive. Marriage in God's eyes is, 'till death do us part'. The union of husband and wife is used to illustrate the covenant relationship God has with each of us who know Him as Saviour. Surely the Christian, knowing something of this 'union with Christ', must view seriously the vows made in marriage, and seek to see the marriage relationship fostered and strengthened in obedience to God's commands.

Nowhere in God's Word do we see that God condones divorce. Only on the grounds of adultery was it permitted. Throughout scripture, sin in general is characterized as spiritual adultery. (See Hos. 2:2; Jer. 3:9; 13:27.)

Just as the 'mixed' marriages of Malachi's day destroyed unity and frustrated God's divine purposes, so today such a situation breeds dissension and unhappiness. 'Can two walk together except they be agreed?' And if there isn't spiritual harmony between parents, what chance does the family stand?

We can glimpse a little of this disharmony and heartache in the life of Sarah. She urged her husband to have a child by her maid. Then she hated the child – her husband's and not her own and she hated the child's mother even more. Can you imagine the quarrelling and strife as those two women tried to live under the same roof? Read about it in Genesis chapters 15-17.

When we understand something of the heartbreak caused by unfaithfulness in marriage, we glimpse a little of God's heartache when His children are unfaithful to Him. How He yearns over us! He said to Israel, 'I longed to gather you as a hen her chicks – but you would not' (Matt. 23:37).

How is your relationship with God?

'My beloved is mine and I am His
And His banner over me is Love.' – (see Song of Solomon 2:16)

STUDY 10
THE QUESTION OF GIVING

QUESTIONS

DAY 1 *Malachi 1:7-8; Leviticus 22:21-23.*
a) What kind of offering would God not accept?
b) What can we offer which is unacceptable (2 Sam. 24:22-25)?

DAY 2 *Acts 5:1-11.*
a) What did Ananias and Sapphira agree to do?
b) To whom did they lie?
c) What happened to them?

DAY 3 *Malachi 3:8-10; Acts 20:35.*
a) Discuss ways in which we can rob God.
b) How can we bring gifts into God's 'storehouse'?
c) Share some of the blessings you have received from giving.

DAY 4 *Malachi 3:10-11; John 15:5.*
a) What two things does God ask us to do here?
b) What will God do in return? (See also Joel 2:25-27)
c) Discuss the two kinds of fruitfulness mentioned in these verses. (See also Gal. 5:22-23)

DAY 5 *Romans 12:1.*
a) What offering above all others, does God long to have?
b) Why?

DAY 6 *Malachi 1:14; Ecclesiastes 5:4-5.*
a) What does Malachi 1 verse 14 say about a person who breaks his vow to God?
b) Is it right to make promises of this kind to God?

DAY 7 *1 Corinthians 16:2; 2 Corinthians 8:1-3.*
a) What can we discover about how the early Christians gave money?
b) Read 2 Corinthians 8:9. What was the supreme example of giving?

NOTES

There is nothing legalistic on this issue of 'giving to God'. The Old Testament pattern of giving one tenth of one's income goes away back beyond the time of Moses.

Genesis 14:20 tells us that Abraham gave tithes to Melchizedek.

Leviticus 27:30-33 shows that the Mosaic law required tithing of all lands, produce and herds. This provided a living for the Levites.

Leviticus 27:31 tells us there were penalties for cheating in tithing.

Many Christians today continue to give a tenth of their income to God and know the blessing of God as a result.

However, the New Testament does not stipulate the amount a Christian should give, but it does tell us a lot about how to give.

We are to give:

Secretly	Matthew 6:3, 4, 18.
Cheerfully	2 Corinthians 9:7.
Freely	Matthew 10:8, etc.

Someone has said, 'Shall we give less under grace than we did under law?' In other words, why stick legalistically to giving just a tithe? Let us give liberally, with cheerful and willing hearts. Why? Because God's Son gave Himself completely in order to redeem us. He longs, not just for our gifts, but that we will give ourselves, all we have and all we are, ungrudgingly to Him.

It is often easier to give money than to give ourselves or our loved ones to God. Look up I Samuel 1:27-28; 2:20-21. Hannah gave up the son she had long waited for, to serve the Lord in His temple. And Hannah and Elkanah were blessed.

God says to us through Malachi, 'Prove me now' ('Test me in this' NIV). Put God to the test and you, too, will know God's outpoured blessing, in such abundance that you will scarcely be able to cope with it!

ANSWER GUIDE

The following pages contain an Answer Guide. It is recommended that answers to the questions be attempted before turning to this guide. It is only a guide and the answers given should not be treated as exhaustive.

NOTES FOR LEADERS

This book sums up much of the history of the Old Testament. Just as John 3:16 is called the 'little gospel', so we might describe Malachi as the 'little Old Testament'. Malachi is a bridge between the Old and the New Testaments. If you read Malachi 3:1 you will see that the 'Messenger' spoken of is the same person mentioned in John 1:23 and Luke 3:3, 4. But a silence of 400 years lies between the voice of Malachi and the voice of one crying in the wilderness, 'Prepare the way for the Lord' (NIV).

Look at the last few verses of Malachi and Revelation. Do you see that the Old Testament closes with a 'curse' and the New Testament with a blessing?

The Jews had been back in Jerusalem after their captivity in Babylon for about 100 years when Malachi, the last prophet to speak to Israel in her own land prophesied. The initial enthusiasm with which the Israelites had re-entered their land had spent itself. Following a period of revival (see Neh. 10:28-39) the people had become religiously cold and morally lax.

It is in this climate that Malachi, the reformer, rebukes and seeks to encourage Israel. He ministered to a people who were perplexed in spirit and whose faith in God seemed to be in danger of collapse. If they were not already hostile to Jehovah, they were becoming sceptical. Malachi, which means 'Messenger of the Lord' was the voice of God, very much as John the Baptist said he was – preparing the way for the coming of the Messiah.

The sins of the Priests
In the first two chapters we discover that the priests had become irreverent and neglectful. Malachi rebukes them for offering worthless animals to God instead of an 'animal without blemish' (Exod. 12:5, etc.). They had lost sight of their high calling in God. They had become greedy for personal gain. So God's condemnation begins with the leaders (Mal. 2:1-9). If the priests did not measure up to God's

high and holy standards how could the people do so? The people no longer kept themselves apart from heathen nations; mixed marriages were commonplace and some men even divorced their Israelitish wives to make this possible (2:10-16).

The sins of the People
The Jews declared that Jehovah didn't love them (1:2). They could not see that His love had provided abundantly for them. Social sin was on the increase (3:5). They became religiously indifferent (3:7). But amidst all the hypocrisy there was a remnant who still feared God and remained faithful (3:16). Malachi longed to develop a strong body of enthusiastic believers who would be able to influence the nation's future. Chapter 3:16 says that God bent His ear to hear His people speak. We find Malachi rebuking their sins one by one:

Ch.	1:6-8	Dead ritualistic worship.
	2:10-12	Evil association.
	2:17; 3:7-8	The questioning of Jehovah's justice.
	3:7-12	Robbing God.
	3:13-15	Impatience.

If we stop and consider, we will realise that we, too, are often guilty of the same sins. Israel was reluctant to confess the sin and failure that existed. Malachi encourages them by assuring them of God's wonderful love. Turn to it and seek to memorise it – Malachi 3:7, 'They shall be mine saith the Lord of hosts, in the day that I make up my jewels; and I will spare them as a man spareth his own son ...' (AV).

God can be depended on to forgive the repentant sinner. Read the story of the prodigal son in Luke chapter 15. This a picture of the forgiving heart of God. The key that opens the windows of God's big blessings is our recognition of His ownership. 'Bring ye all the tithes...' (Mal. 3:10). The giving of a tenth of all we have, time, talents, possessions etc., is the outward recognition that everything belongs to God. He wants us, every bit of every one of us, body, soul and spirit. When we yield to Him like that, He cannot but bless us.

God's message through Malachi was 'I have loved you....' He says that to us today too, so the message of Malachi is for the here and now:

'Back to God's House!
Back to God's Word!
Back to God's Work!
Back to God's Grace!'

Look at the wonderful promise of our coming King in Malachi 3:16; 4:2-3.

GUIDE TO STUDY 1

DAY 1
a) My messenger.
b) The Word of the Lord.
c) Israel. (The whole nation).

DAY 2
a) 'I have loved you' the Lord tells them.
b) 'How have you loved us?'
c) In His love He had chosen them in the days of Jacob (whose name was changed to Israel).

DAY 3
a) God knew before Jacob's birth that he would be a cunning schemer, but that he would respond to God (Gen. 32:24-30; Rom. 9:10-15).
b) Esau did not respond – his tears were not tears of repentance (Heb. 12:16-17; 1 Sam. 24:16; 26:21).

DAY 4
a) Those who will not accept God's gift of new life in Christ inherit eternal damnation.
b) This could mean both spiritual and material inheritance.

DAY 5
a) It was laid waste.
b) They were enemies of God's people and had rejected God.

DAY 6
a) He was just. Those who reject God's love and laws must reap the consequence.
b) We should feel glad and honoured because we don't deserve His love.

DAY 7
a) They saw His might and power to those outside Israel.
b) We shouldn't when we consider what Christ has suffered for us (Isa. 53; Matt. 27:46).
c) No; but He has promised us strength to overcome trials.

MALACHI • ANSWER GUIDE

GUIDE TO STUDY 2

DAY 1   a) His employer. His father.
b) By their attitude to God's laws and wilful offering of blemished sacrifices. Their spiritual decline put Israel on the downward path.

DAY 2   a) Read Hosea 4:9 in the Living Bible, 'Like priests, like people – because the priests are wicked the people are too. Therefore will I punish both priests and people for all their wicked deeds.'
b) By outward reverence when the heart relationship with God is not right.

DAY 3   a) By rejecting Christ's death and refusing to seek the cleansing of His blood, i.e., participating in the 'memorial feast' with sin in our lives.
b) They brought diseased animals as offerings (i.e. tried to deceive God).
c) The offering of an imperfect gift would bring disgrace and possible punishment on the giver.

DAY 4   a) Our attitude of heart, not the value of our gift, is more important to God.
b) A 'godly' person or church fellowship.
c) Yes, God has promised, and will hear and answer a cry for forgiveness.

DAY 5   a) They were insincere and disobedient to His Word.
b) Willing and wholehearted service.

DAY 6   a) From East to West; from every tribe, language, nation and race.
b) The prayer of God's people.
c) In the name of Jesus our Lord and Saviour.

DAY 7   a) Personal.
b) Personal.
c) Personal.

GUIDE TO STUDY 3

DAY 1
a) Lack of reverence and taking God's name on our lips lightly. God will punish this and show people that He is Holy.
b) They scoffed at the table and offerings because they were not right with God. They didn't get their share of the meat offered as sacrifices because the meat wasn't fit to be eaten.
c) Personal.

DAY 2
a) Vows should not be lightly made. Better not to make a vow than break it.
b) It certainly was not.
c) God's name is to be honoured and feared in all the earth. Those who love and serve Him should so glorify God by their lives that others will want to do the same (see Ezek. 36:23 in King James version).

DAY 3
a) To bring glory to God. (This happens when we love and obey Him.)
b) If we are truly born again we should be serving our Master, Christ.
c) Because they, like the priests, must set God's standards before the people.

DAY 4
a) Their children.
b) Banishment from God's presence.
c) The 'upright'; those who please God.

DAY 5
a) The priests were given the laws and commandments, and were to teach the people. NB The 'commandment' ('admonition' NIV) of v. 4 refers to the warning given in vv. 3-4.
b) Yes, this is why God calls people into His service, to feed others with His Word according to their spiritual need and maturity, i.e., milk for babes, meat for the strong.
c) He was to teach the Word of God to those who wanted to follow Jesus.

DAY 6
a) True instruction, the absence of anything false.
b) It is very important to practise what we preach. Paul shrank from being inconsistent and earnestly desired that he would live out

what he taught.

DAY 7   a) Because God has called us to be holy, like Himself.
b) 'Sham' Christians, i.e. people who don't 'ring true', Christians
who say one thing and act another.
c) God wants us all to communicate His message of salvation, by
life and lip, to those who do not know Him.

GUIDE TO STUDY 4

DAY 1   a) It is definitely a contradiction of God's Word for a Christian to marry a non-Christian.
b) Division in the home. Issues where the Christian has to compromise. Difficulty of church affiliation where children are concerned, etc., etc.

DAY 2   a) No, the Word of God directs otherwise – the marriage vow is 'till death do us part'.
b) So that His people would not be drawn away from Him into heathen nations.

DAY 3   a) Because the people had broken God's laws. (They were not what they seemed to be.)
b) Because it means broken vows and promises.

DAY 4   a) When two become one in marriage only death should break this relationship.
b) Children of a broken marriage do suffer and it is difficult as a 'single' parent to train and discipline a child in God's ways.

DAY 5   a) People 'twisted' the Word of God to suit their own ends.
b) We can be blind, stubborn or 'know-all' in our own worldly wisdom rather than take God at His Word and obey Him.

DAY 6   a) Yes, a just God must deal with sin.
b) He has made provision for us to become 'new creatures' in Him, and made a way by which we can be constantly cleansed from sinning.

DAY 7   a) Personal.
b) Personal.

GUIDE TO STUDY 5

DAY 1   a) John the Baptist: Prepare the way for the coming of Christ.
b) Fill the temple with His glorious presence.
c) Yes, the Christian's body is called a 'temple of the Holy Spirit'.

DAY 2   a) Scripture leaves us in no doubt. There is no second chance. We either make our peace with God now or suffer judgement when Christ comes.
b) God tests us in the trials and problems of life so that we will be 'proven gold'.

DAY 3   a) To work in the temple, offer sacrifices, intercede for the people.
b) In the giving of ourselves in loving service to Him, in praising God, in praying and communicating His love to others, etc.

DAY 4   a) The priests were ordinary men and needed to have God's cleansing and forgiveness too.
b) He wants us to yield our whole body and life to Him in willing service.

DAY 5   a) They see the Temple in Jerusalem as all-important – Jesus taught that it is how and not where we worship that is important.
b) They are all an 'abomination unto God' – things that will separate us from the Lord.
c) They will be cast into the lake of fire – will be eternally cut off from God.

DAY 6   a) Judge him.
b) 'Godly fear' is an attitude of heart which acknowledges that we reverence and respect God and desire to walk righteously before Him.

DAY 7   a) They all show that God does not change.
b) No.
c) God cannot break His Word or, Christ died in vain.

GUIDE TO STUDY 6

DAY 1 a) By spending selfishly and neglecting our duty to give to God for the work of His Kingdom.
b) Tithes, the giving of the tenth part of all that God gives to us, are in acknowledgement of all God's goodness to us. Tithing is but the beginning of giving. Offerings are what we freely give over and above the tenth.

DAY 2 a) God's judgement falls on those who don't obey Him.
b) God blesses and loves a cheerful giver.

DAY 3 a) They were to bring their gifts to the Temple to be used in the support of the Levites who served in the Temple.
b) They are prospered and blessed of God beyond all limits.

DAY 4 a) God gives so abundantly that we are overwhelmed with His generosity, i.e., He didn't just send a few drops of rain, but opened the 'windows of heaven' and poured out a deluge!
b) Personal.

DAY 5 a) He will make them fruitful and productive by destroying the things that prevent growth.
b) God's purpose is to make our lives fruitful and productive for Him.

DAY 6 a) The locusts utterly destroy the crops and leave the ground barren, but God will make the desert to blossom like a rose so that surrounding nations will see how blessed His people are.
b) The God of heaven and of all those who belong to and worship Him.

DAY 7 a) If they had been walking closely with God they would not have been complaining about Him.
b) Because one day we will be called to account for all the unprofitable things we have said which may have grieved God's heart and hurt His children.

GUIDE TO STUDY 7

DAY 1
a) The first verse shows a people at variance with God, the second a people in harmony with God.
b) They felt the heathen, who knew nothing about serving God, were blessed more than they were.
c) Psalm 1 shows clearly that those who walk in His ways will be eternally blessed; those who do not, will be eternally damned.

DAY 2
a) No one can be really happy without the Lord even although they get some pleasure out of life.
b) They may heap up temporal riches, but spiritually they are poverty-stricken. Those who love and serve God are laying up 'treasure in heaven' (Mark 10:21).

DAY 3
a) Their talk was of the Lord and His blessings.
b) It should be 'second nature' to Christians to be talking of the Lord and His goodness to them and not wasting time with idle chatter.
c) Personal.

DAY 4
a) See also Exodus 32:32. All who trust in Christ as Saviour are written in His book.
b) Personal.

DAY 5
a) If you are a Christian then you belong wholly to Christ. Christians no longer live to please themselves, but to do God's will.
b) When He comes again.

DAY 6
a) Those who love and serve the Lord.
b) The righteous who reverence, serve and speak about God. The unrighteous (wicked) who despise God's service and speak evil of Him.

DAY 7
a) The day when Christ will come again to receive His own and judge the world.
b) They will be beyond God's grace and suffer the 'second death'. (See notes for fuller comment on this.)

GUIDE TO STUDY 8

DAY 1   a) Personal.
b) Personal. Maybe a reluctance to accept the idea of final punishment. Maybe a new eagerness to see friends coming to know the Lord.

DAY 2   a) To those who obey Him.
b) The sun, with healing rays (Amplified Bible 'Beams of light').
c) Like calves set free! Absolutely free from all that bound us. Like Christ himself.

DAY 3   a) Those who fear and reverence the Lord.
b) No, God has His appointed time for His verdict to fall.

DAY 4   a) Yes, the Ten Commandments do hold for today.
b) Because they are moral laws which have never been rescinded.

DAY 5   a) John the Baptist.
b) To repent and turn back to God.

DAY 6   a) Fathers and children.
b) He was greater that any man who ever lived.

DAY 7   a) After the sin of Adam and Eve.
b) Thorns and thistles appeared for the first time.
c) Not until the New Heaven and New Earth come.

GUIDE TO STUDY 9

DAY 1
a) Yes. The Lord loves us, but we can turn away from Him.
b) A Marriage. We are united with Christ.

DAY 2
a) To the Lord.
b) It is a common temptation for young Christians to enter into marriage with partners who do not know the Lord.

DAY 3
a) Because their lives were sinful; they were disobeying God.
b) Their tears were 'crocodile' tears. They were sorry for themselves, not sorry they had grieved God. They were unwilling to pay the price of putting their lives right and living in obedience to God.

DAY 4
a) Separating from their Jewish wives and marrying others.
b) The Bible underlines the importance of the marriage vows and does not condone divorce except on the grounds of adultery.

DAY 5
a) Because he had taken his brother's wife.
b) Philip, her husband, was still alive and therefore their marriage vows were binding.
c) So seriously that the punishment in Old Testament days was death.

DAY 6
a) No. All sin is sin against God.
b) As soon as we acknowledge our sin and confess it to Him we are forgiven because of our claim on Christ's sacrifice.

DAY 7
a) He said that the one without sin was to start stoning her. (Death by stoning was the penalty for adultery.)
b) They were convicted of being guilty of sin.

GUIDE TO STUDY 10

DAY 1   a) An animal which was not healthy and unblemished.
b) A gift that costs us nothing.

DAY 2   a) They decided to keep back some of the money for themselves.
b) They really lied to God, the Holy Spirit (vv. 4, 8).
c) They died and fear came upon the church.

DAY 3   a) By neglecting to use our income, time, etc., as God wants.
b) Support His work and His workers through churches, missions, etc.
c) Personal.

DAY 4   a) Bring our tithes and offerings and prove Him.
b) Pour out blessing on us and our land.
c) I. Produce from the ground. 2. Fruit from our lives.

DAY 5   a) Ourselves.
b) He wants to use us in His service.

DAY 6   a) 'Cursed' is the one who breaks his vow. The opposite of blessing – divine judgement comes on him.
b) Better not to make a promise than to break it; but if we keep our hearts right with God we will want to do all He requires and more.

DAY 7   a) They put aside money for God's work on the first day of the week and they gave generously.
b) The Lord Jesus, who, though He was rich, became poor for our sakes.

THE WORD WORLDWIDE

We first heard of WORD WORLDWIDE over 20 years ago when Marie Dinnen, its founder, shared excitedly about the wonderful way ministry to one needy woman had exploded to touch many lives. It was great to see the Word of God being made central in the lives of thousands of men and women, then to witness the life-changing results of them applying the Word to their circumstances. Over the years the vision for WORD WORLDWIDE has not dimmed in the hearts of those who are involved in this ministry. God is still at work through His Word and in today's self-seeking society, the Word is even more relevant to those who desire true meaning and purpose in life. WORD WORLDWIDE is a ministry of WEC International, an interdenominational missionary society, whose sole purpose is to see Christ known, loved and worshipped by all, particularly those who have yet to hear of His wonderful name. This ministry is a vital part of our work and we warmly recommend the WORD WORLDWIDE 'Geared for Growth' Bible studies to you. We know that as you study His Word you will be enriched in your personal walk with Christ. It is our hope that as you are blessed through these studies, you will find opportunities to help others discover a personal relationship with Jesus. As a mission we would encourage you to work with us to make Christ known to the ends of the earth.

Stewart and Jean Moulds – British Directors, **WEC International**.

OTHER TITLES AVAILABLE IN THE WEC BIBLESTUDY BOOKLETS

OLD TESTAMENT

1-85792 885 7
Messenger of Love
A study in Malachi

1-85792-888-1
Triumph over Failures
A study in Judges

0-90806-755-0
A Saviour is Promised
A study in Isaiah 1-39
John Priddle

0-90806-706-2
Hypocrisy in Religion
A study in Amos
Marie Dinnen

0-90806-728-3
The Beginning of Everything
A study in Genesis 1-11
Marie Dinnen

0-90806-751-8
Unshakeable Confidence
A study in Habakkuk and Joel
A. Bakes

THEMES

1-85792-892-X
God's Heart, My Heart
What the Bible Says about World
Mission

0-90806-739-9
Finding Christ in the Old Testament
A Study in Pre-existence and
Prophecy
Dorothy Russell

0-90806-720-8
Freely Forgiven
A study on Redemption
Marie Dinnen

0-90806-702-X
Freedom You Can Find it!
Marie Dinnen

0-90082-880-3
Understanding the Way of Salvation
Carol Jones

CHARACTERS

1-85792-887-3
Abraham-A study in Genesis
A Study in Genesis 12-25

1-85792-889-X
Serving the Lord
A study in Joshua

1-85792-890-3
Focus on Faith
A Study of 10 OT Characters

0-90806-761-5
The Cost of Obedience
A Study of Jeremiah
Dorothy Russell

0-90806-746-1
A Man After God's Own Heart
A study of David
Esma Cardinal

0-90806-700-3
God Plans for Good
A study of Joseph
Dorothy Russell

0-90806-707-0
Achieving the Impossible
A study of Nehemiah
Dorothy Russell

NEW TESTAMENT

1-85792-886-5
The Worlds Only Hope
A study in Luke

1-85792-891-1
Walking in Love
A Study in John's Epistles

0-90806-736 4
The Early Church
A study in Acts 1-12
Esma Cardinal

0-90806-7216
Made Completely New
A Study in Colossians and
Philemon
Dorothy Russell

0-90806-716-X
Jesus-who is he?
A Study in John's Gospel

0-90806-701-1
Faith That Works
A study in James
Marie Dinnen

A full list of over 50 'Geared for Growth' studies can be obtained from:

ENGLAND *North East/South*: John and Ann Edwards
5 Louvaine Terrace, Hetton-le-Hole, Tyne & Wear, DH5 9PP
Tel. 0191 5262803 Email: rhysjohn.edwards@virgin.net
North West/Midlands: Anne Jenkins
2 Windermere Road, Carnforth, Lancs., LA5 9AR
Tel. 01524 734797 Email: anne@jenkins.abelgratis.com
West: Pam Riches Tel. 01594 834241

IRELAND Steffney Preston
33 Harcourts Hill, Portadown, Craigavon, N. Ireland, BT62 3RE
Tel. 028 3833 7844 Email: sa.preston@talk21.com

SCOTLAND Margaret Halliday
10 Douglas Drive, Newton Mearns, Glasgow, G77 6HR
Tel. 0141 639 8695 Email: mhalliday@onetel.net.uk

WALES William and Eirian Edwards
Penlan Uchaf, Carmarthen Road, Kidwelly, Carms., SA17 5AF
Tel. 01554 890423 Email: penlanuchaf@fwi.co.uk

UK CO-ORDINATOR
Anne Jenkins
2 Windermere Road, Carnforth, Lancs., LA5 9AR
Tel. 01524 734797 Email: anne@jenkins.abelgratis.com

UK Website: www.wordworldwide.org.uk